MW00368313

55 ART SONGS

COMPILED AND EDITED BY

SIGMUND SPAETH

AND

CARL O. THOMPSON

New and original translations by

SIGMUND SPAETH

A book for unison choral singing, for class or individual teaching, and amateur and professional singers, at home or on the concert stage.

————————•◄◆►•————————

Copyright © 1943 by Summy-Birchard Music
a division of Summy-Birchard Inc.

All rights reserved.   Printed in U.S.A.
Copyright renewed 1970

ISBN 0-87487-082-8

Summy-Birchard Inc.

exclusively distributed by
Warner Bros. Publications Inc.

15800 N.W. 48th Avenue
Miami, Florida 33014

FOREWORD

THIS book is a cross section of the entire literature of Art Song. Every one of the 55 numbers is a classic of its kind and each is by a different composer, which in itself makes the collection unique.

The selections are all art songs in the best sense of the term, showing the individual characteristics of their creators, with the music closely following and clearly interpreting the text, even in the conventionally strophic form, and with piano accompaniments usually of independent musical value. These accompaniments are not too difficult for the average player, nor do the vocal parts require any unusual range, volume or technique.

The book is intended for unison choral singing, for class or individual teaching, and for amateur or professional singers, at home or on the concert stage. It has been made as practical as possible, with texts, translations and arrangements particularly adapted to school and college use, but also aimed at all those who are interested in the great songs of the world.

The idea of such a collection was first suggested by Carl O. Thompson, head of the Division of Fine and Applied Arts at the State Teachers College, Bemidji, Minnesota.

Mr. Thompson had found by experience that mixed choruses often like to sing in unison, thus giving everyone a chance at a real melody, and that such numbers could actually be included in concert programs, in addition to their value for practice and recreation. The nucleus of our comprehensive list came from his own experiments as a choral conductor, and the appeal of this material to both students and teachers can thus be guaranteed in advance. Community choruses will also unquestionably welcome such a contribution to their repertoire.

While the songs inevitably speak for themselves, the editors are inclined to stress a few points as worthy of note. The wide variety of mood and content is fairly obvious, from a frankly popular tune like Tosti's *Goodbye* or Sullivan's *Lost Chord* to the religious inspirations of Schubert and Beethoven. A gratifyingly large number of the songs (18 in all) were written originally to English texts, including the immortal words of Shakespeare and other poets. The best of the old English composers, from Thomas Morley to Sir Henry Bishop, are represented, while America contributes the work of our earliest songwriter, George Washington's friend, Francis Hopkinson, the unforgettable Edward MacDowell, and the beloved Stephen Foster, whose *Open thy Lattice, Love,* was not only his first publication, but perhaps the only work in his long list that could strictly be called an art song.

Many of the numbers provide excellent material for vocal training, as in the flexibility required by Carey's *Pastoral* or Gounod's *Sing, Smile, Slumber,* the volume and range of Schubert's *Omnipotence* or Beethoven's *Glory of God in Nature,* the legato of *Passing By* or *My Lovely Celia,* the accurate intonation stressed in so modern a piece as Moussorgsky's *Cradle Song to the Poor,* and the clear enunciation demanded by Morley's lively *Now is the Month of Maying* or Becker's ecstatic *Days of Spring.*

Some of the words are undeniably sentimental (as what song writer is not?), and there are occasional expressions of gloom, relieved by the steadfast calm of Bach's one love-song, *If Thou Art Near,* written for his wife. But there are also many touches of humor, most surprisingly in such classics as Pergolesi's *Se tu m'ami* and Martini's *Plaisir d'Amour.*

Off the beaten track is the charming *Boat Song* of Grieg, as well as Liszt's *It Must be Wonderful Indeed,* Haydn's *She Never Told Her Love* and Tschaikowsky's *At the Ball.*

Actually there is not a weak song in the entire collection. It is hoped that singers will find in this book the same pleasure that was experienced by the editors in assembling and arranging its contents.

Sigmund Spaeth

A Note on the Translations

THE value of this book to singers, teachers and students is greatly enhanced by the new translations contributed by Dr. Spaeth. He has infallibly caught the original atmosphere and meaning of these songs and has chosen English words that are consistently expressive and remarkably well adapted to the melodic line.

It is no exaggeration to say that in many cases this collection presents for the first time truly singable translations of the masterpieces of German, French, Italian and Russian art song. Wagner's *Träume,* the Strauss *Morgen,* Franz's *Widmung* and Cornelius' *Ein Ton* stand out as revelations of the possibilities of the Lied in our own language, and the subtleties of such French texts as *Beau Soir,* *L'Heure Exquise* and *Psyché* have perhaps never before received such fitting expression in English. For individuals as well as for group singing in unison, these translations should prove both a practical help and an artistic delight.

Carl O. Thompson

TABLE OF CONTENTS

Now Is the Month of Maying

Music by THOMAS MORLEY (1557-1602)
Piano arr. by Roy S. Stoughton

1. Now is the month of May-ing, When mer-ry lads are play-ing.
2. The spring, clad all in glad-ness, Doth laugh at win-ter's sad-ness. Tra la
3. Fie, then, why sit we mus-ing, Sweet youth's de-light re-fus-ing?

la la la la la la la la la, La la la la la la la.

Each with his bon-ny lass A-dan-cing on the grass,
And to the bag-pipe's sound, The nymphs tread out their ground, La la
Say, dain-ty nymphs, and speak, Shall we play bar-ley break?

la la la, La la la la la la la, la la la la la.

Come Again, Sweet Love

JOHN DOWLAND (1562-1626)
Piano acc. by Roy S. Stoughton

Not too slowly

1. Come a -
2. Come a -
3. Out a -

gain, sweet love doth now in - vite Thy gra - ces
gain, that I may cease to mourn, Through thy un -
las! my faith is ev - er true, Yet will she

that re - frain To do me due de - light.
kind dis - dain: For now left all for - lorn,
nev - er rue, Nor yield me an - y grace.

To see, to hear, to touch, to kiss,
I sit, I sigh, I weep, I faint,
Her eyes of fire, her heart of flint

to die, With thee a-
I die, In dead-ly
is made, Whom tears nor

gain in sweet-est sym - - - -pa - thy.
pain and end-less mis - - - -er - y.
truth may once in - - - -vade.

The Silver Swan

Words by
CHRISTOPHER HATTON

Music by **ORLANDO GIBBONS** (1583-1625)
Piano arr. by Sigmund Spaeth

Larghetto

The sil-ver swan who, liv-ing, had no note, When death ap-proach'd un-lock'd her si-lent throat. Lean-ing her breast a-gainst the reed-y shore, Thus sang her first and last and sang no more: "Fare-well, all joys! O death, come, close mine eyes; More geese than swans now live, more fools than wise."

When To Her Lute Corinna Sings

Words and Music by
THOMAS CAMPION (1575-1619)
Piano acc. by Roy S. Stoughton

Andante con moto *(Not fast)*

1. When to her lute Co - rin - na sings,
2. And as her lute doth live or die,

Her voice re - vives the lead-en strings,
Led by her pas - sion, so must I.

And doth in high-est notes ap-pear
For when of pleas-ure she doth sing,

As a - ny chal - lenged ech - o clear: But when she doth of mourn-ing speak, E'en
My thoughts en - joy a sud-den spring: But if she does of sor - row speak, E'en

with her sighs, her sighs, her sighs the strings do break, the strings do break.
from my heart, my heart, my heart the strings do break, the strings do break.

Bid Me To Live

Words by ROBERT HERRICK

Music by HENRY LAWES (1595-1662)
Piano acc. by Roy S. Stoughton

1. Bid me to live and I will live Thy pro-tes-tant to be; Or bid me love, and I will give A loving heart to thee.

2. A heart as soft, a heart as kind, A heart as sound and free As in the whole world thou canst find That heart I'll give to thee.

3. Bid that heart stay, and it will stay To hon-or thy de-cree; Or bid it lan-guish quite a-way, And't shall do so for thee.

Come Unto These Yellow Sands

Words by WILLIAM SHAKESPEARE
From "The Tempest"

Music by HENRY PURCELL (1658-1695)
Piano arr. by Roy S. Stoughton

Come un-to these yel - - - low sands And then take hands:

then take hands: Foot it feat-ly here and there And, sweet sprites, the

bur-then bear. Hark, hark! The watch-dogs bark! Hark, hark! I hear The

strain of chan-ti-cleer, Hark, hark! I hear The strain of chan-ti-cleer.

My Lovely Celia

Piano arr. by Sigmund Spaeth

Words and Music by GEORGE MONRO
(1680? - 1731?)

Passing By

Words from Thomas Ford's Collection
(1607)

Music by EDWARD PURCELL (1689-1740)
Piano arr. by Roy S. Stoughton

Andante con moto

1. There is a la - dy sweet and kind, Was nev — er
2. Her ges-tures, mo - tions and her smiles, Her wit, her
3. Cu - pid is wing - èd and doth range Her coun - try,

face so pleased— my mind; I did but see her
voice my heart — be - guiles, Be-guiles my heart, I
so my love — doth change; But change the earth, or

pass - ing by, And yet I love her till I die
know not why, And yet I love her till I die.
change the sky, Yet will I love her till I die.

ten. *rit.* *D.C.*

Blow, Blow, Thou Winter Wind

WILLIAM SHAKESPEARE
from "As you like it" (abridged)

THOMAS AUGUSTINE ARNE (1710-1778)
Piano acc. by Roy S. Stoughton

1. Blow, blow, thou win-ter wind,__ Thou art__ not__ so un-kind,__ Thou art not so un-kind As man's in-grat-i-tude.
2. Freeze, freeze, thou bit-ter sky,__ Thou dost__ not__ bite so nigh,__ Thou dost not bite so nigh As ben-e-fits__ for-got.

Thy tooth is not so keen,__ Be-cause thou art not__
Tho' thou the wa-ters warp,__ Thy sting is__ not so__

A Pastoral

Piano acc. by Roy S. Stoughton

Words and Music by
HENRY CAREY (1690? - 1743)

Flocks are sport - ing, Doves are court - ing,
Flocks are bleat - ing, Rocks re - peat - ing,

War - bling lin - nets sweet - ly sing.
Val - leys ech - o back the sound.

Ah! _____

Joy and pleas - ure, With - out meas - ure
Danc - ing, sing - ing, Pip - ing, spring - ing,

Kind - ly hail___ the glo - rious spring,
Naught but mirth___ and joy___ goes round,

Kind - ly hail the glo - rious___ spring.
Naught but mirth and joy___ goes___ round.

Love Has Eyes

Words by CHARLES DIBDIN
(1745-1814)

Music by SIR HENRY ROWLEY BISHOP
(1786-1855)

Beneath a Weeping Willow's Shade

Piano acc. adapted from the original by
Roy S. Stoughton

Words and Music by
FRANCIS HOPKINSON (1737-1791)

The mock-bird sat up - on a bough, The

mock-bird sat up - on a bough And lis - ten'd to her lay, —— Then

to the dis - tant hills he bore The dul - cet notes a - way, —— Then

to the dis - tant hills he bore The dul - cet notes a - way, —— The

dul - cet notes a - way, —— The dul - cet notes a - way. —— way. ——

I've Been Roaming

Words by GEORGE SOANE

Music by CHARLES EDWARD HORN (1786-1849)

Andante con moto

I've been roam-ing, I've been roam-ing Where the mead-ow dew is sweet, And I'm com-ing, and I'm com-ing With its pearls up-on my feet. I've been roam-ing, I've been roam-ing Where the mead-ow dew is sweet, And I'm com-ing, and I'm com-ing With its pearls up-on my feet. I've been roam-ing, I've been roam-ing O'er the

rose and lil - y fair, And I'm com-ing, and I'm com-ing With their

blos-soms in my hair. I've been roam-ing, I've been roam-ing Where the

mead-ow dew is sweet, And I'm com-ing, and I'm com-ing With its

pearls up-on my feet. I've been roam-ing, I've been roam-ing Where the

hon-ey-suc-kle creeps, And I'm com-ing, and I'm com-ing With its

Blow High, Blow Low

Words by CHARLES DIBDIN

Music by CHARLES DIBDIN (1745-1814)
Piano acc. by Roy S. Stoughton

Blow high, blow low! let tem-pest tear The main-mast by the board. My heart, with thoughts of thee, my dear, And love well stored, Shall brave all dan-ger, scorn all fear, The roar-ing wind, the rag-ing sea. In __ hopes on shore to be once more Safe __ moor'd with thee.

2. A - loft, while moun-tains high we go, The whis-tling winds that scud a - long, And the

surge roar-ing from be-low, Shall my sig - nal be to

think on thee, Shall my sig_nal be to think on thee, And this shall be my

song: 3. And on that night, when all the crew, The mem-'ry of their for-mer lives O'er

flow-ing cans of flip re-new, And drink their sweet-hearts and their wives.

I'll heave a sigh, I'll heave a sigh and think of thee. And as___ the

ship rolls thro' the sea, The bur-den of my___ song shall be:

Open Thy Lattice, Love

Words by GEORGE P. MORRIS

Music by STEPHEN COLLINS FOSTER
(1826-1864)

Allegretto

1. O_pen thy lat-tice, love, lis-ten to me! The cool balm-y breeze is a-
2. O_pen thy lat-tice, love, lis-ten to me! In the voy-age of life love our

broad on the sea! The moon like a queen roams her realms of blue, And the
pi - lot will be! He will sit at the helm wher-ev-er we rove___ And

stars keep their vi-gils in heav-en for you. Ere morn's gush-ing light tips the
steer by the lode-star he kin-dled a-bove. His shell for a shal-lop will

hills with its ray, A - way o'er the wa-ters, a - way and a-way! Then
cut the bright spray, Or skim like a bird o'er the wa-ters a-way.

o-pen thy lat-tice, love, lis-ten to me! While the moon's in the sky and the breeze on the sea.

It Was a Dream

English Words by
FREDERICK H. MARTENS

Music by
EDUARD LASSEN
(1830-1904)

The Lost Chord

Words by
ADELAIDE A. PROCTOR

Music by
SIR ARTHUR S. SULLIVAN
(1842-1900)

Seat-ed one day at the or-gan, I was wea-ry and ill at ease, And my

fin-gers wan-dered id - ly O - ver the nois - y keys; I

know not what I was play-ing, Or what I was dream-ing then, But I

seemed the har-mon-ious ech- o From our dis-cord-ant life; It linked all per-plex- ed meanings In-to one per-fect peace, And trem-bled a-way in-to si - lence, As if it were loth to cease. I have sought but I seek it vain-ly, That one lost chord di - vine, Which came from the soul of the or - gan, And en - tered in - to mine. It

may be that Death's bright An - gel Will speak in that chord a -

gain; It may be that on - ly in Heav'n I shall hear that grand A -

men. It may be that Death's bright An - gel Will speak in that chord a -

gain; It may be that on - ly in Heav'n I shall hear that

grand A - men.

The Sea

Words by WILLIAM DEAN HOWELLS

Music by EDWARD A. MacDOWELL, Op. 47, No. 7
(1861-1908)

in vain, Man-y and man-y a year.— But the state-ly wide-winged

ship lies wrecked, Lies wrecked on the un-known deep;— Far un-der, dead in his

cor-al bed, The lov-er lies a-sleep,— Far un-der, dead in his

cor-al bed, The lov-er lies a-sleep,———— a-sleep.—

Good-bye

Words by G. J. WHYTE-MELVILLE

Music by F. PAOLO TOSTI
(1846-1916)

Fall-ing leaf and fad-ing tree, Lines of white in a sul-len sea, Shad-ows ris-ing on you and me, Shad-ows ris-ing on you and me; The swal-lows are mak-ing them read-y to fly, Wheel-ing

cord is fray'd, the cruse is dry, The link must break and the lamp must die.—

Good-bye to Hope! Good-bye, good-bye, Good-bye to Hope! Good-bye,

good - bye.——— What are we wait - ing for?

Oh! my heart! Say fare-well to me now———

— and part! A - gain,——— a - gain!——— my heart,—

Sunrise on the Ganges
(Gia il sole dal Gange)

English version by Sigmund Spaeth   ALESSANDRO SCARLATTI (1649-1725)

If Thou Love Me
(Se tu m'ami)

English translation by Sigmund Spaeth

Music by GIOVANNI PERGOLESI
(1710-1736)

If thou_ love me,— if thou be sigh_ing, dy - ing for_ me, shep-herd true,— Then I grieve for all thy suf-f'ring, Thy fond love should have its due.— Yet_ think not that thou a - lone art cho -sen as my fav - 'rite swain. Gen-tle shep-herd, be ad-vis-ed, One may light-ly love a-gain; Gen-tle shep-herd, be ad-vis-ed, One may light-ly

love a-gain, One may light-ly love a-gain. Luscious ros-es, crim-son flam-ing,

Syl-via may pre-fer to-day, Yet, their thorns im-pa-tient blam-ing, On the mor-row

fling a-way, On the mor-row fling a-way. Men may think that girls— are sil-ly,

Need I hum-bly grant their pow'rs? Just be-cause I love the lil-y, Must I scorn all

oth-er flow'rs?

The Joy of Love
(Plaisir d'amour)

English translation by Sigmund Spaeth

Music by GIOVANNI MARTINI
(1741-1816)

The joy of love_____ may not have long to stay, _____ But all through life runs the sor - row of love's dis - may! I say fare - - well to the whims of my

Syl - via's heart, She has al - read-y made an-oth - er start! The joy of love____ may not have long to stay,____ But all through life runs the sor-row of love's dis - may!____

Ah, Love of Mine
(Caro mio ben)

English translation by Sigmund Spaeth

Words and Music by GIUSEPPE GIORDANI
(1744-1798)

Ah, love of mine,

Canst thou di-vine How, far from thee, my heart must grieve?

Canst thou di-vine How, far from thee, my heart must grieve?

Faith-ful to thee, sighs that I heave Pray that to me thou

45

If Thou Art Near
(Bist du bei mir)

English translation by Sigmund Spaeth

Music by JOH. SEBASTIAN BACH
(1685 - 1750)

thus should be end - ed, To know that thy dear hands shall be there, My

trust-ing eyes at length to close. What joy that life thus should be end - ed,

To know that thy dear hands shall be there, My trust-ing eyes at length to close.

If thou art near, then I go glad - ly To meet my death in calm re -

pose, to meet my death in calm re-pose.

rall.

She Never Told Her Love

Words by WILLIAM SHAKESPEARE
in "Twelfth Night"

Music by JOSEPH HAYDN
(1732-1809)

Largo assai con espressione

She nev-er told her love, She nev-er told her

love, But let con-ceal - ment, like a worm in the

bud, Feed on her dam - ask

Lullaby

(Wiegenlied)

Author unknown
English translation by Sigmund Spaeth

Music by WOLFGANG AMADEUS MOZART
(1756 - 1791)

1. Sleep, lit-tle dream-prince of mine, Leave your toy sol-diers in
2. All in the house is quite still, Sun has dropped o - ver the
3. Lit - tle prince, are you a - ware That you are free from all

line. Birds have all gone to their nest,
hill. Flow - ers and trees are a - sleep,
care? Dream-ing of can-dies and toys,

E - ven the bees are at rest; Heav - en - ly stars and the
Shad-ows lie heav - y and deep. An - gels are watch-ing a -
Liv - ing for in - no - cent joys, All of us wait-ing on

moon All will be greet-ing you soon,
bove, Guard-ing your cra - dle with love;
you, Proud of the ser - vice we do,

Thro' the dark night they will shine.
Heav'n sends a bless-ing di - vine.
Such a sweet life must be fine.

Sleep, lit-tle dream-prince of mine. Sleep on, sleep on.

The Lotus Flower
(Die Lotosblume)

Words by HEINRICH HEINE
English translation by Sigmund Spaeth

Music by ROBERT SCHUMANN, Op. 25, № 7
(1810-1856)

Larghetto

The lo - tus flow'r is anx - ious

When the hot sun shines bright, And with her droop-ing chal-ice She

Omnipotence
(Die Allmacht)

Music by FRANZ SCHUBERT
(1797 - 1828)

English translation by Sigmund Spaeth

Great is Je - ho - vah, the Lord! _____ For Heav'n and the

earth both pro - claim a - loud _____ His might. Great is Je-ho - vah, the

Lord! For Heav'n and the earth both pro-claim a-loud His might. In

Now His might in the thun-der is heard, It flames in the light-ning, swift des-cends in the flood! Yet clear - est of all — in our beat - ing hearts we can feel Je - ho - vah's might, yet clear - est of all we feel in our hearts Je - ho - vah's might, the Lord ____ in His glo - - ry! Then in

Dedication
(Widmung)

Words by MÜLLER

English translation by Sigmund Spaeth

Music by ROBERT FRANZ, Op. 14, No. 1
(1815-1887)

Andante espressivo

Oh, thank me not for songs I bring thee,

My thanks far more should go to thee. Thine was the

gift,___ I do but sing thee What thine a - lone shall

al - ways be. Thine are the songs we love so

dear - ly, The light___ of thy dear eyes in mine

Help'd me to read them, true___ and clear - ly,

Dost thou not know___ these songs___ are thine?___

Dost thou not know_____ these songs___ are thine?___

The Glory of God in Nature
(Die Ehre Gottes aus der Natur)

Words by ANDREAS HOFER

English translation by Sigmund Spaeth

Music by
LUDWIG VAN BEETHOVEN
(1770-1827)

1. The heav'ns are telling the Lord's end-less glo - ry, Their sound rings out His Ho - ly Name. The earth and sea com-bine in the sto - ry, That man may hear what gods pro - claim. Who

2. Be - hold and see all the works of cre - a - tion, That Na - ture hath for us un - furl'd. Does not this or - der make pro-cla - ma - tion Of one great Lord who rules this world? Canst

bears the stars that de-fy all our count-ing? Who
thou ig - nore all of life's count-less treas-ure, O'er-

brings the sun to light each day? It comes and
look the small-est grain of dust? To Him who

shines with its broad laugh-ter mount-ing And like a he - ro goes its
made this give praise in full meas-ure And put in Him a - lone your

way,___ And like a he - ro goes its way.
trust,___ And put in Him a - lone your trust.

On Wings of Song
(Auf Flügeln des Gesanges)

Words by HEINRICH HEINE   Music by FELIX MENDELSSOHN BARTHOLDY

English translation by Sigmund Spaeth   (1809-1847)

Andante tranquillo

1. On wings of song thro' dream - land My love a - far I bear, Off to a flow'-ring stream - land, O - a-sis of beau - ty rare. There blos-soms in gar-dens are throng - ing, The

vio - lets gay and smil - ing Look up at stars shin-ing clear, Soft-ly the ros-es be-guil - ing To fra-grant words give ear. The list'-ning ga-zelles come bound - ing, A -

moon shines clear— a - bove,_____ And lo - tus flow'rs are
wait _ ing si-lent the dawn,_____ And in the dis - tance

long — ing To win their sis - ter's love,_____ And
sound — ing The sa - cred stream flows on,_____ And

lo - tus flow'rs are long - - - ing To
in the dis - tance sound - - - ing The

win their sis - ter's love.
sa _ cred stream flows on.

It Must Be Wonderful Indeed
(Es muss ein Wunderbares sein)

Words by REDWITZ
English translation by Sigmund Spaeth

Music by FRANZ LISZT
(1811-1886)

It must be won-der-ful in-

deed, Two hearts their love re - veal - ing, In all so

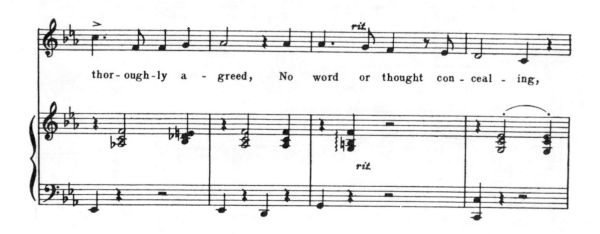

thor-ough-ly a - greed, No word or thought con - ceal - ing,

Dreaming
(Träume)

Words by MATHILDE WESENDONCK
English translation by Sigmund Spaeth

Music by RICHARD WAGNER
(1813-1883)

Ah, what won-der lies in dream - - - ing!

p
animated
pose, Dream - - - - ing, as when rays of glo - ry, On the
pp
cresc.
mf
Ped.
p ritenuto
bliss-ful spir-it fall-ing, Pic-ture one e-ter-nal sto - ry, All for-got-ten,
dim.
pp
cresc.
f a tempo
p
one re-call - ing, Dream - - - ing, as when Spring would cap-ture From the
accel.
f
p
Ped.
snow each blos - som sweet, That with ne'er sus-pect-ed rap-ture Then the morn-ing sun would
cresc.
dim.

Monotone
(Ein Ton)

English translation by Sigmund Spaeth

Words and Music by
PETER CORNELIUS (1824 - 1874)
Op. 3, No. 3

What won-drous tone is in the air? My heart can hear it ev - 'ry - where. Is it the sigh, the fin-al breath, Be-fore thy lips were closed in death? Is it the tol-ling of the bell, That sad-ly rang thy fune-ral knell?

So clear and strong I hear it roll, As tho' it held thy ver - - y soul, _____ As tho' thy love were still ex- press'd And sang my bit-ter grief to rest. _____

74

Alone in the Fields
(Feldeinsamkeit)

Words by H. ALMERS
English translation by Sigmund Spaeth

Music by
JOHANNES BRAHMS (1833-1897)
Op. 86, No. 2

Slow

I lie quite still in grass so green and high, My sweep-ing glance a - bove thro' space far send - ing, far send - ing, While myr-iad in-sects hum a - cross the sky, And heav - en's blue seems won-drous-ly un-end-ing, And heav - en's blue seems won-drous-ly un -

The Days of Spring
(Frühlingszeit)

Words by MIRZA - SCHAFFY
English translation by Sigmund Spaeth

Music by REINHOLD BECKER
(1842- 1924)

Not too fast: with joyful expression

When the signs of spring can first— be seen, And the sun comes out to melt the snows, When the trees dis_play___ a touch of green, And a - mid the grass___ a flow -'ret shows, When 'tis plain to see that all sud - den-ly There is

no more win-ter gloom to be, ___ Hear it from the height! Hear the

val - ley ring! Oh, how won-drous bright are the days of spring! Oh, how

won-drous bright are the days of spring, the ___ days of spring!

spring   That our hearts to-geth-er sang a   song?   When we

knew that we were queen and   king,   And to   us the world would soon be -

long?   Then all   na - ture sang   and   the wel-kin rang, Then all

na - ture sang   and   the wel-kin rang, As new   life from hill and val - ley

Still as the Night
(Still wie die Nacht)

English translation by Sigmund Spaeth

Music by CARL BOHM (1844-1920)

Still as the night, deep as the sea, Thus is thy

love to be! Still as the night and

deep as the sea, Thus is thy love, thy love to

be, Thus is thy love to be.

Tomorrow
(Morgen)

Words by JOHN HENRY Mac KAY
English translation by Sigmund Spaeth

Music by RICHARD STRAUSS, Op. 27, No. 4
(1864 - 1949)

To-mor-row will the sun a-gain___ be shin-ing   And on the path - way that our foot- steps fol-low will bring us joy a-gain,   Our souls en-twin-

My Native Land
(Gesang Weylas)

Words by EDUARD MÖRIKE

English translation by Sigmund Spaeth

Music by HUGO WOLF
(1860 - 1903)

Adagio e solenne

This is my na-tive land, from far____ off gleam-ing!

The sea is pour-ing on thy sun-ny strand A mist____ that o-ver cheeks of gods

___ is stream-ing. Age-less the wa-ters mount____ a-bout thy youth-ful slopes for-

ev-er free!____ Be-fore thy god-head bow-ing comes

Roy-al-ty thy hum-ble guard to be.

Last Night

Words by CHRISTIAN WINTHER

Music by HALFDAN KJERULF
(1815-1868)

Allegretto

1. Last night the night-in-gale woke me, Last night when all was still, It sang in the gold-en moon-light, From out the wood-land hill. I o-pened my win-dow so gent - ly, I looked on the dream-ing dew, And oh! the bird, my dar-ling, was sing-ing, Sing-ing of you, of you.

2. I think of you in the day-time, I dream of you by night, I wake and would you were here, love, And tears are blind-ing my sight. I hear a low breath in the lime - tree, The wind is float-ing through, And oh! the night, my dar-ling, is sigh-ing, Sigh-ing for you, for you.

3. Oh, think not I can for-get you, I could not if I would, I see you in all a - round me, The stream, the night, the wood. The flow-ers that slum-ber so gent - ly, The stars a - bove the blue, Oh, heav'n it - self, my dar-ling, is pray-ing, Pray-ing for you, for you.

Boat Song
(Im Kahne)

Words by WILHELM KRAG
English translation by Sigmund Spaeth

Music by EDVARD GRIEG, Op. 60, № 3
(1843-1907)

Allegretto grazioso

1. Sea - gulls, sea - gulls in white clouds flock - ing in bright ___ sun - shine!
2. Loos - en, loos - en, my love, thy tress - - es shin - - ing bright!
3. Rock me, rock me on white - capp'd wa - - ter borne ___ a - bove!

Each lit - tle duck with its yel - low stock - ing neat and fine!
Then let us dance in the warm and star - ry sum - mer night!
Sweet-ly there comes like a sea - god's daugh-ter my own true love!

Row,   row   to fish - er's strand,   Qui - et wa - ter is
Wait,   wait on Saint John's day   There'll be wed-ding and
Dream, dream,'tis fate's de - sign,   Thou art mine and

near   the land,   All   the sea ly - ing still, oh!
dance so gay,   Fid - dles play - ing their fill, oh!
I   am thine!   Fid - dles now all are still, oh!

poco rit.   a tempo   D.S.

Ho! wil - low, wil - low!
Ho! wil - low, wil - low!
Ho! wil - low,   wil - low!

Songs My Mother Taught Me
(Als die alte Mutter)

Words by ADOLF HEYDUK

English translation by Sigmund Spaeth

Music by ANTONIN DVOŘÁK, Op. 55, No. 4

(1841 - 1904)

Andante con moto

When our— dear old— moth - er's voice

Train'd us— all in— sing - -ing, She could

scarce with - hold the tears From her eye - lids

wring - - ing.

Now with child - ren all our own, We in

song are train - - ing, Oft the tear - drops

deep well - ing, Fall un - heed - ed down our own cheeks

rain - ing.

Sing, Smile, Slumber

Serenade

Words by VICTOR HUGO

Music by CHARLES GOUNOD
(1818-1893)

1. When thou sing -
2. At thy smile ____
3. In thy slum -

- est when nest-ling at eve   close by my   side, ____
- on thy lips bud-ding love   breaks in-to   bloom; ____
- ber, while fond-ly mine eye   guards thy re - pose, ____

Dost thou know____   what my soul   un - to   thine would fain   con -
Ev-'ry   doubt ____   is dis-pell'd, naught but trust in my soul   finds
And thy lips ____   all un - con - scious to   me   thy love   dis -

fide? ____
room, ____
close, ____

Thy sweet voice wakes the
Ah, thine in - no - cent
When I   gaze on thy

94

Florian's Song
(Chanson de Florian)

Words by CLARIS DE FLORIAN
Trs. by Cordelia Brooks Fenno

Music by BENJAMIN GODARD
(1849-1895)

Allegretto

1. Oh, have you seen a - mong the vil - lage lads
2. If with his plain-tive notes of sweet-ness rare

A shep-herd wise and fair as May? To know him is to love him
He charms the wood-land ech-oes clear, If when he pipes his dul-cet

well, And love him deep-er ev - 'ry day. He is my love,
notes The pen-sive maid-en stops to hear,

Bring him to me, His heart is mine, My faith has he!

The Slave
(L'Esclave)

Words by THEOPHILE GAUTIER
English translation by Sigmund Spaeth

Music by EDOUARD LALO
(1823-1892)

Andante non troppo

A cap-tive slave___ with no friend to be car-ing, I dream___ of young love and its ways.___ Of joy-ous days,___ Ah, joy-ous days!___ And thro' the cold bars blank-ly star - - ing, Numbed in spir - it, on fly - ing birds a-far I gaze!___

Elegy
(Elegie)

Words by LOUIS GALLET

English translation by Sigmund Spaeth

Music by JULES MASSENET
(1842-1912)

Sadly and slowly

Oh,— love-ly spring long a-go,

When all was green, Why is the world now so drear? Heavn's blue no

long - er I know, No more se - rene Bird songs of glad-ness I

hear. Why should my joys all de-part?—— What has the

Psyche

Words by PIERRE CORNEILLE
English translation by Sigmund Spaeth

Music by EMILE PALADILHE
(1844-1926)

Andante quasi andantino

I suf-fer jeal - ous-y   at Na-ture's love for

Psy - che!   Ev-'ry kiss of the sun____ to her is far   too kind,   And her

hair feels too oft the ca-ress of the wind,   Such bold at - ten-tions will dis-tract the

mind! And ev - en when she breathes the air,___ it is fill'd with de-

light To be al-lowed such bless - ing, And the gar-ments a-bout her

press-ing! And the gar-ments a-bout her press-ing! When she sighs it does not a-

gree, I find the prob-lem quite dis-tress-ing, Ah, 'tis eas-y to see That her

sighs are not for me!___

102

Peaceful Evening
(Beau Soir)

Words by PAUL BOURGET
English translation by Sigmund Spaeth

Music by CLAUDE DEBUSSY
(1862-1918)

Un - der the set-ting sun wa-ters blush like the ros - es,

From the breeze comes a trem-bling to the fields of grain,

Peace-ful eve-ning a world of hap-pi-ness dis-clos - es E'en to

hearts that are fill'd with pain. Hold-ing

Exquisite Hour
(L'Heure exquise)

Words by PAUL VERLAINE
English translation by Sigmund Spaeth

Music by REYNALDO HAHN
(1875-)

Tranquillo e dolce possibile

The moon-light blanch - es On trees a - round, From all the branch - es There comes a sound, Na-ture en-hanc - ing. Oh, night en - tranc - ing! The pond's re -

After a Dream
(Après un rêve)

Words by ROMAIN BUSSINE

English translation by Sigmund Spaeth

Music by GABRIEL URBAIN FAURÉ (1845-1924)

Op. 7, No. 1

The Asra
(Der Asra)

Words by HEINRICH HEINE
English Translation by Sigmund Spaeth

Music by ANTON RUBINSTEIN
(1829 - 1894)
Op. 32, No. 6

Moderato (♩ = 76)

Dai - ly walked the love - ly daugh - ter of the Sul - tan in the gar - den, When 'twas eve - ning by the foun - tain, where the wa - ters white are play - ing; Dai - ly stood the youth - ful cap - tive when 'twas eve - ning by the foun - tain, Where the glist - 'ning wa - ters white are

play - - ing. Ev-'ry day the slave grew pal - er,

pale and pal - er. Then one day the Sul-tan's daugh - ter

hail'd the slave with rap-id ques - tion: "What's thy name? I wish to

know it, and thy home-land and thy kin-dred". And the slave re-

At the Ball

Words by A. TOLSTOY
English paraphrase by Sigmund Spaeth

Music by P. TSCHAIKOWSKY, Op. 38, No. 3
(1840-1893)

In midst of the danc - ing en - tranc - ing, I caught but a glimpse of your face, But look-ing so drear - y, so wea - ry, Of hap-pi-ness hard-ly a trace! The mu-sic was whirl - ing and swirl - ing, Your voice came but faint-ly to me, I thought I heard

laugh-ter there-aft – er, Like waves of the tur-bu-lent sea.

It sound-ed so cold and so heart-less, Yet lin-ger-ing still in my

ear, What once had been ten-der and art – less Now

fill'd me so strange-ly with fear! At night when so wea-ri-ly,

sad – ly, I sought for my soul to find rest, A vi-sion came

ee - ri - ly,   mad - ly,   The   ghost of a   love un - ex -

poco meno mosso

press'd!   That vi - sion is   lin - ger - ing,   ev - er haunt - ing,   I

know not the   false or the   true;   Your voice and your

smile may be   taunt - ing,   I   know that I   love on - ly   you!

Tempo I

Cradlesong of the Poor

Words by NEKRASSOFF
English version by Sigmund Spaeth

Music by MODEST MOUSSORGSKY
(1839 - 1881)

Lull-a - by, —— by,

lull-a - by, —— by, Like a mod-est flow-er

in the field, Lit-tle one, too young to know,

What shall be your life's pro - tect-ing shield? Who can tell how you shall grow?

The Nightingale and the Rose
(Eastern Romance)

Words by KOLTZOFF
English translation by Sigmund Spaeth

Music by N. RIMSKY-KORSAKOFF
(1844-1908)

Thus on the harp a min-strel plays And sings his long-ing to the maid, Who, like the rose, is wrapped in si-lence, And know-ing not for whom he sings, Nor why his song is fill'd with grief.

Slumber Song

Words by N. LERMONTOFF
English version by Sigmund Spaeth

Music by A. GRETCHANINOFF
(1864-   )

Andantino: *dreamily*

Sleep, my ba - by, soft - ly dream - ing,

Lull - a - lull - a - by, lull - a - lull - a - by. Gen - tle moon on

cra - dle gleam - ing, Watch - es from the sky.

largamente

No — more need — for songs and sto - ries, Hear — your sleep - y

ten.   a tempo

sigh!   Close — your eyes like morn - ing glo - ries,

poco rit.   a tempo   tardo   rall.

Lull - a - lull - a - by,   by,   by,   by,

a tempo

by.

INDEX BY COMPOSERS